There's A Jewel In You
Volume 1

FROM A STATISTIC TO A SUCCESS

Edited by
Stephanie L. Williams

Greater Working Women Publishing
Columbia, SC
2017

Authors

Shakkyra Austin
Joy Avery
Ronda Braden
Shennice Pruitt-Cleckley
Tammie Jackson
Ashley Thomas
Nefertiria Toussaint
Chanistie Wiley
Calandra Williams
Chantea Williams
Charley Willis

This book is dedicated to every young mother. Don't give up. It won't always be this hard. Success is still in your future. We are all rooting for you to WIN! You are STILL SOMEBODY!

There's A Jewel In You, Volume I

Email requests to info@greaterwomen.com

Ordering Information:
Quantity sales. Special discounts are available on quantity purchases by corporations, associations, and others. For details, contact the publisher at the email address above.

Orders by trade bookstores and wholesalers. Please contact publisher at email address above.

Greater Working Women
PO Box 291764
Columbia, SC 29229
www.greaterwomen.com

Printed in USA

First Printing, 2017

ISBN-10: 0-9991975-0-9
ISBN-13: 978-0-9991975-0-9

TABLE OF CONTENTS

I Am Still Somebody™

FOREWORD

The beautiful outcome of nature's design, one irritating grain of sand can cause an iridescent, lustrous pearl to form. A precious and priceless jewel is developed from a grain of worthless dirt. Dirt is usually overlooked, devalued and swept away. Who wants dirt in their life? Who would think something so worthless could produce a priceless jewel. Well, what I learned at a young age is life will throw dirt your way, but in the end we all have value and there is a priceless jewel within us.

Just as pearls come in a variety of shapes, sizes, and colors, so do people and the kinds of trials thrown into our lives. Becoming a mother at a young age, with no experience or knowledge on raising a family was crazy, but it's my story. I was a fatherless daughter being raised by a single mother in a family full of many examples of all the test and trials of life. What did I know about being a good mother? Then on top of that I became a wife.

I was a young mother with daddy issues trying to be a successful adult, mother and wife. The tragedies of our lives can help us grow, break us down or completely destroy us. Like many young mothers who are just trying to find their way, we devalue ourselves and as a result, lose motivation, insight and value. Like pearls, we all have to go through a process. The process of learning from our mistakes, owning our truth and walking in our God given purpose. We develop a process to protect ourselves from further damage, layer by layer, becoming stronger and more resourceful just like a pearl. A precious jewel.

Regardless of how our stories began, we own the pen and the paper to our future. Recognizing the collective value of our strengths is like wearing our pearls. So regardless of how these ladies stories began they made the choice to activate change and power. Not just for them but for their families and for their future.

DeAnna Bookert

INTRODUCTION

The life of a single, young mother can be very challenging. You may not be sure if you're mothering right. You may second guess yourself on decisions and you may often become stressful from the demands of taking care of a little one. All of this is normal for any mother regardless of age but it increases when you are a teen mother.

In this book you will read the stories of other women who have already walked the road and came out on top. Each story is unique, heartfelt and intriguing with one central theme, "Giving Up Is Never An Option!" No matter how many difficulties you may face, you have to decide within yourself to persevere through it all. The truth of the matter is that your child needs to see you succeed, because you are setting the standards for them. You can go from a statistic to a SUCCESS if you are willing to put in the work.

This book has two main purposes outside of being a best seller. First, it is to encourage, empower and equip young mothers to reach their full potential in life. Secondly, it is to prevent young girls from walking down this path of motherhood before they are married. Our transparencies in the stories to follow about our journeys as young mothers will take your emotions on a rollercoaster. We entered motherhood from the ages of 15-21, but we didn't make excuses. We made moves! Please understand this one important thing, your current circumstances do not determine your destiny. Keep pressing forward until you see greater, because *There is a Jewel in You*!

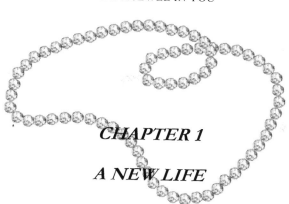

CHAPTER 1

A NEW LIFE

Starting something new usually, begins with training. When I learned to ride a bike, I was given training wheels. When I got new breasts, I was given a training bra, but on a cold November evening, while walking around the hospital in excruciating pain with my boyfriend by my side, I realized, none of the free classes I took or the books that I read had trained me to become someone's mother.

I still had the mind of a child then, full of hope, dreams, and great expectations. I thought my family would come and support me. I thought people would bring me flowers and shower me with gifts. I thought my boyfriend would sleep in my private room and help me with the baby. What actually happened was I walked around a dirty hospital for hours and gave birth flat on my back in a cold and sterile room. I watched him and his friends pass out cigars as they left the hospital to go party at a nightclub to celebrate me giving birth.

When we took our baby home, we did everything that we could to make life great for him. His father was on board and took a day shift, while I took a night shift so that our baby had 24-hour care. It was difficult caring for an infant; he was a new life with wide eyes and great lungs. I had to learn how to rock a baby, how to deal with diaper rash, how to feed him properly, how to catch his moods and be his comforter. I was over-protective; I didn't want anyone to hold him or take over because I was determined to be a good mom on my own. I read many books and watched videos on how to care for a baby, but trial and error taught me the most. At first, his father helped, but he was young, and I wanted a lot from a boy who had barely graced the door of manhood.

As for my relationship with my son's father, immaturity kept us in a constant state of contention. There were arguments over everything from food choices to the music that we would play in the car. As time went on, he started seeing other girls, while we were still together, and this completely shattered my psychology at the time. I thought that we would become the Huxtables and I could not fathom him being with anyone else. Before long, our differences turned destructive and he moved out. After the breakup, he became unavailable to help me and just like that night in the hospital I was alone with my son unsure of my next move.

Though I had an apartment through public housing, I wanted more for us. I decided to work at a daycare across the street so that I could take my baby to work with me and I wouldn't need a car. As soon as I made a few dollars, my food stamps were cut and my rent and utilities spiked. I thought the only way to make it was to either make more money or to get a man to help me. So, I started going to school to make more money and while in school I met a man who promised to help me, and as a bonus, he was in ministry so I married him.

Instead of helping, he controlled me. He wouldn't work consistently, and he was very violent toward me. I never told anyone because I was embarrassed to admit that although we were in ministry, we couldn't make our marriage work. For 13 years we rode a rollercoaster of feast and famine. Things were great and then they were horrible. I published a book in 2005, but my husband was so jealous that he wouldn't allow me to go anywhere to market my book. After seeing my dream come to fruition, I had to let it die because he said so.

I began suffering chest pains and migraines, which were diagnosed as anxiety attacks. After my youngest two children were born, I came to myself and realized that my life was never going to change without help. I began to seek God for a new direction because a life of fear and torment was not what I wanted.

The Bible reads in 1 John 4:4 that

Ye are of God, little children, and have overcome them: because greater is he that is in you, than he that is in the world.

I wanted God to deal with him, but he clearly told me in my tattle tale prayers, "You're not his Holy Ghost." God was showing me clearly that if I was to overcome the hell in my life I had to allow Him to fix me. I decided to go back to school and earn my degree. I would get my kids off to school, go for a full day of courses, get home, and do coursework all night. That continued for the next 3 years until I earned my degree. I did schoolwork while living in hotels, living at his moms or living wherever. I had nothing, but the word of

God to help me get myself together.

I attended teacher certification school after I earned my degree. I decided being a teacher would allow me to spend more time with my children than any other careers. I could have chosen a more lucrative path, but I had to balance going after my dreams with what was best for my kids. The year I started my first teaching job, God provided a way of escape from my marriage. My focused and consistent effort brought forth change.

Being a single mother was harder than I expected. The hardest part was the agony I caused myself being so determined to get a man to love me. I begin chasing a dream that a new man would adopt my family, cure my shame, and relieve my pressure. I learned that a man was not a bailout plan. When God sends the man for my life, he will come to join with me in a mission of love for Gods people and not for our own selfish desires.

My kids are all grown today, except one, and somehow without a father or a dime of child support, we continue to flourish. Destiny designed a unique family for me that I am proud of, bruised but not broken, fragmented but complete. In Philippians 1:6, God promised to complete the good work that He began within me, and my life is a testament to Hhis faithfulness.

~Joy Avery

CHAPTER 2

MISSES FIX IT

I was that girl who thought a baby would fix things; it was my belief that somehow having a child to take care of would complete me and fill the longing I carried in my heart. I thought it would rid my heart of pain. The pain that was left behind from my mother, who seldom told me she loved me but, had enough love to give men who beat her. I also thought having a child would take away the pain of a father who favored my sibling more than me. My perception of love was so messed up that I thought if I had a baby, I'd finally have someone who loved me and couldn't leave me. My hurt, my emptiness, my loneliness allowed me to be careless in my actions and my perception. Call me *"Misses Fix It"* because I thought I had all the answers to fix every problem, issue and ache I had.

This feeling of yearning to have a child didn't occur until I was fifteen years old. I remember the event that spurred my life completely out of control. I had been living at my boyfriend's house, whom I shouldn't have been dating in the first place. One night we heard banging at the door. I was petrified to see my two aunts and their friend yelling at me to open the door and let them in. They began to tell me that I needed to get my things and come with them because my mother was in the hospital. All they would tell me is that there had been an accident and I can recall thinking to myself, my mother had a heavy foot and it wasn't a surprise to hear that she had been in another accident. Before I could step out of the door I noticed their hesitation… my aunt's friend turned to me and said, "Baby, let me prepare you." She began to explain to me as gracefully as she could to a fifteen-year old that my mother was in ICU.

She began to tell me that my mother had taken a blow to the head and her brain had swollen to the size of a grapefruit. The doctors cut out a piece of her skull to try to release the pressure. Her eye socket was broken, along with fractures in her jaw. Due to the swelling, my mother was slowly becoming brain dead. I remember for just a split second… forgetting to breathe. I remember seeing my mother, Karen was her name, lying in that bed with all that gauze around her head, tubes in her mouth and machines making noises that I couldn't understand.

I remember the phone call and was informed they were pulling the plug and that my mother was gone. I remember her fighting with him and him saying that if she ever left him, he'd kill her. I remember her being crazy in love with him… so crazy she couldn't see that it wasn't love at all. I remember her choosing him over me time after time. I also remember her smile, her laugh, I remember… her. Even though she seldom said she loved me, I loved her. Losing her allowed me to feel like I needed to replace that space. God allowed me to graduate high school and be somewhat smart the years in between, that is until I met my son's father.

When my son's dad and I met, it was picture perfect or so I thought. He was charming, hardworking, and seemed to get whatever he went after. We were young and as our relationship grew, we partied and enjoyed each other's company. To me, he had a car, a job, seemed to always be dressed fresh to death, what more could I ask for? We had only been officially in a relationship six short months when we both stared down at that test...the second line appeared. Positive! Although, we would be on again, off again, in using contraception, we never truly took the task seriously. I was so consumed in partying and being in love with him, I hadn't even realized I had missed my period until I was hanging up clothes and noticed my unopened pack of tampons. Secretly, I had hoped for this moment and even dreamt of it.

I had no idea that my reality would sign me up for far more than I could imagine. As the scripture says in 1 Corinthians 13:11, "When I was a child I thought as a child..." and I did childish things. As the weeks progressed, reality set in. What would we do? I'm twenty years old and holding down a retail job. I didn't have a car, no place to call my own or to even lay my head. My entire life and care fell into the hands of the boy I called my man, who was still being taken care of by his mother. Although we thought we were "grown", we were very much babies with no real sense of responsibility. Who was going to help me? My mother was not here to show me the ropes of motherhood and my dad couldn't stay out of jail long enough to even get to know me. My support system was slim to none and I immediately thought about all the reasons why I couldn't do this.

Having my beautiful baby boy changed everything, including my relationships, my sense of self, and the way I saw the world. My routine of getting up and going wherever I wanted, became a routine of making sure I had a change of clothes and diapers. The man that I thought would never leave me began to show me his true colors. When we separated, he left me to raise our five-month old son by myself. My son and I shared a room at my aunt's house where I had a job busting table's part time while making minimum wage. I went from the girl that didn't miss a party to a full-time mother who felt like she was drowning. Drowning in fear, shame, and baby milk.

The life that was dealt to me, made me feel that I was going to be another anomaly or a statistic in an online article. Living in that one room with my baby made me realize that although I loved my son dearly, it hadn't fixed the hole inside of my heart. I began going to a church in my old hometown with a friend of mine. That's when my favor began to take place. In those moments, when I sat in the old church pew not quite sure if I even had a relationship with God, I realized that I belonged in His presence. Now I'm not saying that in that moment my life did an 180-degree turn but, I walked out of church every Sunday with more faith. I started praying and reading some scriptures here and there. Nothing consistent, but I wanted to know more about this God that everyone else knew so well. I knew and trusted that He heard my prayers and my late night cries as I held my baby and He did.

Before I knew it, I was given an opportunity to work full time which allowed me to make more money. Taking care of my son and being a good mother pushed me into grind mode. I began working doubles and picking up extra shifts just to tend to his needs and everything began to fall into place. Within months, I was blessed with an apartment and a car. After searching and searching, I found a church home. I took classes and became a certified nursing assistant. God continued to bless me! He took me from the girl who was everything she didn't want to be, to the woman He knew I could be. I won't lie to you and say that in this journey I have been perfect. Remember in the beginning when I told you about *Misses Fix It*, well, she still had a way of popping up and trying to rear her controlling, ugly head. Looking for all the wrong things to fill that void. After all, we know what's best for us right?

My son's father and I thought we could at least try to work things out. By entering into this relationship, I went up against everything God said not to do. Shacking up with someone who still didn't know how to love me right, left me homeless, carless, and pregnant, AGAIN! They say when you continue to do the same thing over and over again expecting a different outcome is insane. I had felt like I had made my bed in insanity. This second time around sent me into a whirlwind of baby blues and depression. I somehow forgot how God had brought me out before and I hadn't grown enough to trust in Him that He would do it again. Now here I was twenty-three with two kids, back sleeping in my aunties' bedroom, no car, no hope and just low.

"*Misses Fix It*" had to go away for good because nothing she had done benefited me. In not trusting God and assuming control over my life, I had made a mess of it. This second time around following God and having His approval was all that I needed. Maybe I didn't know everything after all and that was okay. In acknowledging that, I learned to completely transform my mind and the way I perceived my situation. Instead of looking at my circumstances in a negative light I began to see God in it. Tending to my two children empowered me. Raising them alone as a single mother gave me drive and strength. I want you to walk away with this story knowing that you are built for this. God wouldn't put more on you than you can bear and that you still can succeed.

Today I stand not serving as "*Misses Fix It*" from the outside, but I now look to work with God to fix my emptiness within. I serve an awesome God! I am currently employed full time and a student at the local university pursuing my bachelor's degree in Business Management. I have my own place and car. My son's father and I are working slowly but, surely to co-parent our two boys the right way. I serve as one of my church's outreach leaders and every day I have a reason to smile. I am in the preliminary stages of starting an organization for children who live in households of domestic violence.

God has brought me out of my struggle and continues to work miracles for me. Although I've made the mistake of thinking I could control the reigns in my life and its outcome, life has begun to manifest itself. Being a single mother has not and will not take me out and it won't take you out either! If you struggle with insecurity, voids from your past, and think a baby can fix the pain, I hope that my life's journey is an inspiration to you. I hope that you would take the time and allow God to help you heal. Having a baby before you're ready won't close that empty space for you. If you are the young lady, who has her beautiful child or children already, know that it's already getting better. That you were built strong enough and even though you may have made the wrong choices, those choices don't make you. You can attain everything your heart desires with a little bit of hope, a heaping hand of faith, and a whole lot of fight. Trust me, you will shock the world.

~Shakkyra Austin

CHAPTER 3

MY PAIN BIRTHED PURPOSE

A few years ago no one could have told me that I would become something great. Being the daughter of a well-known preacher, I still found myself pregnant at seventeen. Today, at the age of twenty-eight I am a mother, entrepreneur, motivational speaker and author. I'd like to encourage you on this one thing, "Despite Your Circumstances Live Your Dream."

As a child, I quickly learned that I was placed on a pedestal I never asked to be on, nor did I choose the family I was born into. Living under a microscope was draining. I just wanted to be treated like a normal person and I found myself suffocating when I so desperately wanted to breathe. Why did kids bully me? Why did I have to wear skirts to play sports? What did it mean to have a normal life? Why did I have to share my parents with the church? Why did I have to be molested? Most importantly, why was God so ugly and mean to me? These are some of the questions that I asked myself quite often.

At age sixteen, I ran away from home in search of a void that I would try to fill with a sense of normalcy and acceptance in society. All the questions led me to seek the heart of the one person whose love I could remember and recognize all the way back to the 7th grade. The boy who would become my daughter's father. We attended different high schools but after three years I reconnected with him and we instantly started dating. A month after losing my virginity to him, I became pregnant.

February 6, 2006, was the day I needed my mom by my side more than anything. Instead, I remember getting out of the back seat of the car with my aunt, closing the door and watching my mom drive away. Was I that embarrassing? Was she that ashamed of me? Feeling heartbroken, my aunt and I went to my very first doctor's appointment to confirm that I was in fact pregnant. After hiding my pregnancy for 2 months, the truth was finally revealed. I was definitely pregnant! Despite the obstacles I would face, I was determined to be great. During one of the most crucial times of my life, I felt so rejected. It literally felt like hell on earth. Why was my sin any different than the next? Why was the word "rape" even mentioned? Why did I have to be called, "Hot and Fast"? For several months, I dealt with so much ridicule and persecution. I had to hear my mom say, "If it weren't for you I wouldn't have had to stay on my job longer to keep health insurance on you." Knowing that, made me believe I was nothing more than a financial burden. On the other hand, my dad was silent and didn't say much my entire pregnancy. I knew I let the man that meant the world to me down.

On September 20, 2006, at 1:21 A.M., my life officially changed forever. I was now a seventeen-year-old high school senior, preacher's daughter and now an unwed mother. It was told to me prior that my daughter's dad would not be allowed in the delivery room to see me physically under those conditions. I was 2 weeks overdue and a few hours after being admitted to the hospital, the nurse noticed my daughter's heart rate dropping. I was instantly prepped and taken into emergency surgery. Her father had stayed at the hospital for hours with my two good friends, but he left prior to knowing I'd have to have an unexpected surgery. He was the star fullback of the high school football team. If he arrived late to school the next day he would not have been able to hit the field. We both knew and understood what he was trying to do, to be seen by scouts and potentially receive a full ride scholarship for college, which never happened.

To hear my hollering, pooping baby girl cry for the first time, I was prepared to give life everything that I had. Just when I thought things would get better after arriving home, the heartache became worse. For a couple of months, I was not allowed to take my daughter to see her dad. I was told he didn't need to see her if he couldn't provide for her. Constantly hearing that he needed to man up to support our daughter, became stressful. I knew in my heart he had all the intentions in the world to be a great dad, but over time I allowed the words, "He's a sorry and lazy bum," to fester in my mind until I believed it.

Despite being out of school for two months with the help of the most amazing homebound teacher, Ms. Jordan Pound, I managed to graduate top 24% of my graduating class. Five years later I was walking across the stage again top 10%, this time completing college. During my 2nd year of college, my daughter's father and I broke up. Having a degree was the best feeling in the world, but I wanted so much more for our life. With pure determination to overcome a teen pregnancy and being a single mom, I found myself feeling depressed, insecure and suicidal. It showed up in the relationships I chose, the friends I hung around and my environments. I spent a lot of time living to please others, that I completely lost myself in the process. In 2014, I sought to discover Ashley Nicole Thomas.

After reading, "Rich Dad Poor Dad" by Robert Kiyosaki, I discovered the best investment you could make, is to invest in yourself. April 30, 2015, with just my savings account, I launched Fire Ant Marketing. A year later, I discovered my true purpose that would lead me to my destiny, motivational speaking. It became a driving force to go back into schools and share my story with other teen moms like myself. I wanted to be to teen moms what I wish I had in high school. It's one thing for teachers to encourage and motivate you, but it's another thing to have someone you can physically touch and relate to, that has experienced what you are currently experiencing. I set all fears aside and became my most vulnerable self. Opening up about wounds that I had suppressed so heavily. People saw a belly but they didn't see what I dealt with behind the scenes. It was time for my voice to be heard and for once someone would listen, be blessed and inspired.

I collaborated and trained with a movement in South Africa, called "The World Needs a Father." I then realized where a lot of my hurt and pain derived from. I was searching for my father's love in the bed with other men. I became promiscuous so young, not fully understanding how being molested multiple times at 5 years old had affected me psychologically. When being introduced to menstrual cycles in the 4th grade, I was told to tell my teacher that a period was the dot at the end of the sentence. Completely deprived of learning what I would face as I developed into a young lady. I was never sat down and given the sex talk. Knowing I wasn't taught completely about womanhood and life, I went into the world blind, gullible, naive and educated by the wrong sources.

It was fine and dandy to be taught in church about God and the Bible but I didn't always need church teachings. I needed my parents to be open and real with me about life issues. I was very sheltered from reality. Fully aware of all the many things that influenced and affected my decision-making.

I am learning how to take my wounds, forgive the people and release. With a different perspective, I know my parents raised me to the best of their ability and for that, I am forever grateful. They gave my siblings and I the life they only dreamed of.

To all my beautiful Queens, "I am not my sister's keeper, I AM MY SISTER." I do this for you so that you too can be encouraged to have the same drive and ambition to finish something great. Your child is not a mistake and your life isn't over. Discover your own wounds so that you can heal and progress in life. Every generational curse stops with you. Know that you are beautiful, you are loved, and you are deserving. Remember to have grace, mercy, and understanding for our men. The majority of us mothers are raising children in a fatherless generation. How can we realistically expect boys to be men and men to be fathers and fathers to be husbands, when they themselves most likely didn't have a man nor a father to raise them! They too are wounded, broken, hurt, and angry just like we are.

Queen always remember, "DESPITE YOUR CIRCUMSTANCES LIVE YOUR DREAM."

~Ashley Thomas

It is not what you are called, but what you answer to.

~African Proverb

CHAPTER 4

IT TAKES A VILLAGE...

Becoming a mother at age eighteen after one and a half years of college changed my plan of getting my Bachelor's degree in computer programming and operations to that of full-time motherhood. As the oldest daughter of a family of seven, I helped my mother with my younger siblings' daily care, unknowingly becoming part of their village. Since I had cared for my siblings, my transition into motherhood wasn't as shocking as it might have been for a new mom starting out with no experience on how to handle a baby, what things to expect from a baby, their feedings, and what to do if they cried constantly. Though my mother was a stay at home mom, you can imagine that seven children might be a handful.

I helped with dinner preparation, homework, diaper changing, baths and play time. When my son was born, I still lived at home with my parents and younger siblings. Once I started working, my mom kept him until I got off and then I'd go straight home put on my mommy hat and cape and took over. Though I could have stayed home and collected government assistance, the benefits of sitting at home and barely surviving just weren't great enough to convince me that it was my best option. My mom told me that she would help out by keeping her grandchild while I worked.

As my family grew, I realized that state aid wouldn't be enough to provide the things that I felt my children would need to survive without struggling. My family offered moral support as well as some financial support when and if they could. My grandmother would always talk to me and reassure me to do the best that I could and make sure that I treated my children with love and respect. They loved her to the moon and back and she loved them just as much. She was an awesome woman and they still talk about how well she treated them and loved them to this day.

Since I was used to helping my mother with my younger siblings, the only thing that I had to accept about having a child at eighteen was that I was totally responsible for this handsome infant and his upbringing. As he grew, I found joy in his first steps, listening to his baby talk and the forming of his personality. He was such a bright young man, full of promise and life. I have now reared six awesome children in total, three young men and three young ladies. I wouldn't trade it for anything. It was such an accomplishment to watch and be a part of their growth.

I raised them to be respectful to each other as well as others. It was a great joy to parent them and I am thankful for their village that helped with their upbringing, keeping them if I needed to go to a meeting, the grocery store or just to offer a relief if I was overwhelmed with work. Their teachers also provided additional village support. I made sure they knew I was available to talk at any time for any reason and I didn't think my child was beyond mischief so they didn't have to worry about that. They offered additional resources if needed and encouraged each of the children to do their best and made sure they knew they were somebody.

Mom, I urge you to make sure you make yourself available to the school faculty and administrators. Take advantage of the programs available to support your child's education. Don't just send them to school, visit the school yourself, participate in field trips, parent-teacher conferences, sporting events and be sure to meet the teacher at the beginning of the school year. Also, make sure they do their homework, study, eat a good breakfast and get enough rest.

I didn't feel like I was a statistic, and still don't, truth be told. I have worked for the last 30 plus years to ensure that my children were productive citizens, cared about the next person and didn't become a statistic themselves, with so many things going wrong in society today. They share stories now about how they weren't happy with me when they were growing up because one individual did something, but they couldn't, and how they now understand why I wouldn't agree to everything they thought they wanted to do. It was sometimes challenging to stand my ground with them, especially, if they did or said something that was truly hilarious while I was trying to be serious, but I believe that by the grace of God, we made it.

We had ups and downs during this time, but God saw us through. We faced financial hardships, repossessions, small meals, and even a fire but through it all, it was because of them that I chose not to give up. I knew that God gave me charge over them and I wanted to do right by Him. Someone once told me that my downfall was having six children and I kindly shared with them that if it hadn't been for my children, I might not have made it this far.

They helped me keep my head level and I was there to support them and answer their questions when and if they arose. Growing up as a child, my siblings and I were taught that children should be seen and not heard. Wanting my children to be able to speak to me about any and everything, I developed an open relationship with them very early on to start building their trust. We have an awesome bond and they encouraged me when I finally decided to go back to school and work on my degree.

I strive to be present for every life event that they have. They confide in me and respect my opinions without criticizing what I say. I always try to ask questions that will help them think about the best route to take instead of telling them what to do. It seems that when you tell them what to do outright, they go against each and every word you say. Don't be discouraged, hold on and when needed, call someone from your village.

I feel that my greatest accomplishments were raising my children, helping them become successful adults and allowing them to make their own life decisions. If I had to do it all over again, I would possibly start my family after I completed college, which is one of the values that I instilled in them. I am pleased with my life and I am thankful that I am still here to share my story with teen moms.

I want to encourage the teenage mothers out there to

hold your head up no matter what anyone says. Your child did not ask to be here, but they are depending on you to be there for them and to lead them. It may seem hard and challenging but I encourage you to stand strong and continue to support them. There will be challenges that arise, so gather your village of supporters early. The village is very important to your family's success. Don't wait until you are ready to pull your hair out to ask for help. Let someone know what's going on and seek the village while you are still in control of the situation. When your village tells you the truth about something, don't be offended, hear them out and be open to discussion when and if it arises.

Your children need you and all that you desire to teach them. It will seem like they are rebelling against all that you are trying to teach them, but hang in there and always, always support them and hold them up. Even when you must chastise them, they should know why it is being done. Your desire for their lives should be so great that you just can't allow them to do any and every thing regardless of what their friends or associates are doing. Remember God is holding you accountable for their upbringing. Proverbs 22:6 says, "Train up a child in the way he should go and when he is old, he will not depart from it."

Always seek the best for your children but remember, self-care is also very important. If you aren't alright, you won't be able to make sure your children are alright and have the necessary provisions. Trust yourself and the decisions that you make for your family. Don't try to do everything yourself.

Pay close attention to your child(ren) and their behaviors.

You want to catch situations before they get out of control and discipline when necessary. Just because it's cute, doesn't mean it's right. Know that each child will be different and that you must build a separate relationship with each of them.

My FINAL and MOST IMPORTANT word of advice: NEVER, EVER show favoritism. It can ruin a child's self-esteem, causing them to feel inferior and less important than the favored sibling. It might even lessen your chances of building a trusted relationship with them. Once resentment sets in, it will be very hard for you to regain their trust and they won't hear anything you have to say because they will remember how you treated them and how it made them feel.

~Ronda Braden

CHAPTER 5

THE STRUGGLE

The struggle was real for me as a child. I grew up in the ghetto, surrounded by drugs, alcohol, and prostitution. Growing up, my family was poor. I was raised by my grandmother. My mother was around mostly, but she was living a reckless life. I met my biological father only twice. I witnessed, domestic violence as a child growing up. I never felt like I was loved because my parents weren't around. So I sought love in other people.

I saw this guy that lived one house down from me. He was a little older than me. I thought he was cool. We had sex, and I only gave in because I believed he would like me more. One time I decided not to have sex with him and he punched me in the mouth. I had never physically been abused by a man before. I was in shock, but I was also hurt. I lied for him because he begged me to. The abuse never stopped, it only got worse. Because we were having unprotected sex, I missed my period.

I didn't know how to tell my mother but she suspected that I was pregnant. So she took me to a clinic to take a pregnancy test. At fifteen years old I found out I was pregnant. Devastated, I cried for hours. I was more hurt that I would have to tell my grandmother I was pregnant. I became ashamed of what I had done. I knew an abortion was not an option because of my Christian upbringing. I knew my only choice was to keep the baby and share the news.

I told my family, and they didn't judge me, they supported me. I also told the father, but there was little reaction from him. I had mixed emotions about his response. I couldn't focus on him too much because I still had to finish school.

I was only a freshman in high school. When I went back to school I tried to act normal, but I knew there was nothing normal about being a pregnant teen. Morning sickness was the worst because I couldn't keep any food down. I ate little because I didn't want to gain weight. Most of all, I was trying to hide my pregnancy from my friends. It worked mostly until the news got out I was pregnant. I lost most of my friends. Their parents wouldn't let them talk to me anymore. I was hurt even the more.

During the summer break, I changed schools. There was a school in Downtown Dallas for pregnant teens. My mother transferred me there for my sophomore year. Life seemed easier around other pregnant teens, but it was still weird. I was only a baby having a baby—so embarrassing.

To be honest, I hated the choice I had made in life. I often wished that I could turn back the hands of time. It was too late to dwell. September 25, 2001, I turned sixteen and three days later on September 28, 2001, my daughter was born into the world. She was a bundle of joy, but the fears down on the inside of me overpowered the joy I should have felt. I kept thinking, "How can I be someone's mommy?"

I wanted to have an entire pity party and blame my mother, absent father, and even my grandmother. The fact of the matter was I made a conscious decision to lie down and now I had to make a conscious decision to raise this baby.

I was determined to give her the best life. I kept pressing forward towards the mark. The struggle was real, but I finished high school a year early. I started my first job at seventeen. I had to use government help to get by with the little I was making. I knew this would only be temporary. Every day I rose, focused on being a better version of me. I wanted more out of life so I kept grinding until we made it. I made it out of the ghetto, no longer needed government help, and made enough money to support us. I was told I wouldn't be successful and I would be a statistic. I wasn't supposed to finish high school. I would need government help to survive. My daughter would have a baby out of wedlock. I would only make minimum wage and we would live in poverty.

All of these were lies. I overcame every statistic by the grace of God. I went back to the roots I was introduced as a child. I accepted Christ into my life. Since my decision to accept Christ in my life, my life has been so much better because He revealed my purpose. My story of teen pregnancy gave me the passion for inspiring the next young lady.

Your story may look like its ending but it's only the beginning. God has a plan for you. Don't allow the negative things to be planted down on the inside of you. Say to yourself, "I am still somebody!" There's a jewel in you waiting to shine! You are the light of this world. Your story will inspire millions if you allow your setback to become a setup for your comeback. I'm excited about your future, dear heart!

~Calandra Williams

Silence has a mighty noise

~African Proverb

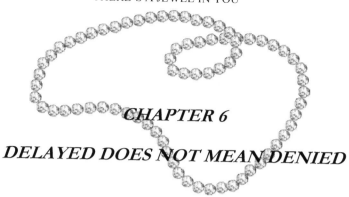

CHAPTER 6

DELAYED DOES NOT MEAN DENIED

Sixteen years old, in the 11th grade and now these folks are telling me I'm about to become somebody's mother. Thinking back now, I'm not sure what was going through my mind when I got confirmation, but I do remember thinking I was going to find my own place, because my mom was going to kick me out when she found out. I gave birth two weeks after my 17th birthday. At that moment I embarked on the most challenging, traumatic, yet rewarding journey of my life. Immediately, I had to deal with all of the negativity that was being spoken to me such as, "Now your life is over!" Being told repeatedly that a baby was NOT a toy, as if I didn't know this already!

As a teen mom, I had many decisions to make. I was fully aware that every decision had to be the right one for me and my son. One thing I was determined to do was to finish high school. I was scared and felt like I would never be a good mother. Every decision I made was overturned by my mother. It felt like I had my son for her. She wanted to control every detail from what I named him to which outfits he wore. I felt a lot of resentment because she never listened to me as a parent. It seemed like she was purposely making things difficult for me just to teach me a lesson or punish me for getting pregnant.

My nights were long and the days at school were longer. I

was transferred to an alternative school called COPE over the summer and I continued there until the second nine weeks of my senior year. Upon returning to high school, things became a little more difficult for me. With it being Senior year, class pictures, all the senior activities, testing and college decisions, I loved school but dreaded going home. If my son was not there, I would not have even wanted to go home. As soon as I walked in from school, all I wanted to do was drop my book bag, grab my son to bond and play with him.

Unfortunately, there was always something else that needed to be done. When certain chores were delayed, I was accused of being lazy or using my "mommy duties" to avoid work. I was made to feel bad about wanting to be a mom to my son. I wanted to fully experience being a MOM to him. I never for once thought I knew everything. However, I knew I wasn't as dumb or naïve as every ADULT made me feel. I never felt any real support for my situation. I was the topic of family jokes, conversations and always used as the prime example of what you "didn't want to turn out to be." I felt alone and imprisoned.

I recall when the college recruiter came to my house to talk to me about college and explain all my options. My mom pretty much insisted on making the decisions for me, when the recruiter was firm about me making my own decisions, my mom became upset. When the topic of housing arose for school, my mom flat out said if I decided to go out of state to college that was fine, but I would not be taking my son. She would fight me in court to keep me from taking him with me. My entire world came crashing down at that moment. I felt that all I had been working so hard for in school, the long hours studying, the struggle of keeping my grades at a 3.8, staying out of trouble, every plan, every goal, and every dream were all for nothing.

I would never leave my son and go to another stat, not even for a weekend. I went into a deep depression and pretty much gave up on any promising future for me and my baby. I left school to get a job, so I could save my money to get my own apartment. I worked, while going to school at night. When the time came for me to move out, my mom locked me out of the house, refusing to give me my son. Though I eventually got my baby from her, she still wanted to control everything I did concerning my child and my life. It was as if she didn't believe I could be a good successful parent unless she was involved or making the decisions. I don't recall her ever encouraging me. I don't recall hearing, "I love you," either. She always made me feel like a complete, worthless failure at everything. Nothing I did was ever good enough. Did I really embarrass her that much? Did she forget that she too became a mother at seventeen?

I only heard complaints and criticism concerning my parenting. Everything I did was wrong in her eyes. Needless to say, the relationship between my mother and I was severely strained. Anything she said to me seemed like darts of poison and not nurturing words of support. I became pregnant again and started the vicious cycle of becoming just another statistic. After my second son was born prematurely and required me being in the hospital for long extended times with him, my mom used his birth as an opportunity to take my oldest son into her custody. I was an unmarried mother of four by the age of 21.

I dealt with a lot of criticism and negative talk, while my dreams and goals were constantly shot down. However, the emotional and mental strain of losing custody of my oldest son pushed me to the edge. I struggled to balance motherhood and continuing my education. I was going through an emotionally, physically, and mentally abusive marriage. There didn't seem to be much support for a young mom with four kids. I was written off and devalued. I was mistreated, often taken advantage of by those who claimed to love me and have my back. I was quickly becoming just another young black woman with a washed-up future. Destined to be on public assistance and sentenced to the bare bottom, scrapping off society to survive. Every day was a struggle. I felt like a failure as a daughter, as a mother, as a wife, and even as a person.

Through this experience, I learned that success was not determined by anyone else's perception of me. Success is defined as the accomplishment of an aim or purpose. It is also defined as a person or thing that achieves desired aims or attains prosperity. My success was not determined by my mom, the kids' fathers, a husband, what society or the masses deemed successful. It was not determined by anyone's critical evaluation of me or my journey. My success was determined by ME!

I had to discover my PURPOSE and define my goals for my life, then put a plan into action to accomplish them. Success didn't come for me until I redefined what being successful personally meant to me. Success for me was getting my kids to and from school daily, providing them with decent meals, properly fitting clothes, and suitable housing. Success was raising them to establish a solid relationship with God and being able to make strong, sound decisions. Success was keeping my kids out of jail, off the streets and alive long enough to become productive yet positive contributors to society. Success was being the best mother to my kids individually, as well as, collectively. Success was also deterring my daughters from repeating the cycle of teen motherhood.

My plans and dreams for myself were temporarily placed on hold so my babies could have a better chance at life. I eventually obtained my GED and enrolled in classes at the community college, while working various jobs. As I grew older, I realized that my mother did her absolute best at parenting me. Babies don't come with manuals. She was responsible for another life and the process of a child before she herself fully understood her own process.

I healed by anchoring myself in God's Word, staying in prayer and learning to live my life to my own expectations. I embraced my PROCESS. Now, nine children and two failed marriages later, I'm finally accomplishing my dreams and goals. I own several small businesses and I'm the founder of two non-profit organizations. I'm a proud mother of five sons, Joseph (29) Joshua (28), Justin (26), Jamal (19) & Ja'mir (13) and four daughters, Dominique (25), Daya (17) and twin girls Da'Kodah (8) & Sapphire (R.I.P). Today, I'm also a pastor, ministry leader and author. Truly I'm living proof that delayed does not mean DENIED. Motherhood is not an easy journey, but it is a very rewarding one. Teenage motherhood IS NOT the period at the end of your story. It is just a chapter of many wonderful promises that God has in store for you. Giving up is NEVER an option. The most expensive and valuable jewels are only obtained after the pressure and strain of the process is applied.

~Tammie Jackson

When a needle falls into a deep well, many people will look into the well, but few will be ready to go down after it.
~African Proverb

CHAPTER 7

SHE SAVED ME

Normally I would cringe at the idea of going back to what I consider the worst chapters of my life. For many reasons, there are parts of my childhood that are still very shameful to me. I've grown to know and understand that my past life experiences are where I learned the most valuable lessons. I will use those lessons to encourage, empower and equip any young lady who is now traveling the same road I once was on. I will do my best to help the misguided realized that they may be headed in the wrong direction.

Growing up I often didn't feel loved, wanted or needed. I got to a point in my life where I was afraid to let anyone in emotionally because it seemed like all I had ever really experienced was hurt, disappointment and embarrassment. For so long I was filled with uncontrollable anger, and agony from being told, "No one will ever want or love you, and you will never amount to anything." In my mind those things were true and I wasn't exactly the product of what my family considered to be great. Both of my parents struggled with their own demons. I felt like I was being punished because of their struggles to gain control of their drug, alcohol addictions and other habits in order to be able to take care of their responsibilities.

Once I felt like I was old enough to make my own decisions, I set out in life in search of love and friendship in all of the wrong places. I knew I didn't belong hanging with an older crowd, but they welcomed me with open arms. They made me feel as though they loved me and they treated me as if I was one of their own. It was during this time of my promiscuity that my daughter's father and I began an intimate relationship. He said and did all the things that I thought were right. It took me some time to recognize just how far off track I had gotten but even then, I was in too deep.

I remember finding out I was pregnant like it was yesterday. I was a freshman in high school at the young age of fifteen. It was January 2005, and I had just come back from a basketball tournament. I told one of my close teammates about how I normally tracked my monthly business but had noticed it had been a few weeks and that wasn't normal for me. I waited a few more days and then decided to sneak and buy myself a home pregnancy test. I ended up taking three. Of course, all of them came back positive. In those moments I cried and cried. I didn't know what to do. I knew I couldn't tell anyone. My promiscuity had finally caught up with me. At this point, I was already a few months, and my plan was to go into labor before anyone could ever find out.

I continued my relationship with my daughter's father as if nothing were out of the ordinary. It wasn't until he figured out that I was pregnant that I had ever thought about admitting to anyone that I was actually pregnant. I didn't really know what to expect once I told my family, but I knew it wasn't going to go well. Once I announced that I was pregnant, I was kicked out of the house and told, "My life was over," and my only option was to have an abortion. I was confused. I was brought up in a Christian home and taught that abortion is a sin. That went against everything I believed in and had been taught to stand for.

Against my will, I was taken to an abortion clinic. I

prayed the whole way there because I didn't want to do it. I was nervous and scared, with a million and one thoughts running through my mind. No, I didn't want to be a teenage parent, having a baby out of wedlock. I had no clue how I was going to raise a child, finish school and do all the things that I had planned out for my life, but I was sure that I couldn't kill my baby. When we arrived at the clinic, we were asked to sign in and have a seat. When I was called to the window and could not present proper identification I was turned away. It was at that very second that I knew my daughter was destined to be here. I didn't realize at the time, but that was the beginning of the process of God's journey to mold and shape me to become the woman I am today.

For the next few months, I dealt with the laughter, constant criticism and shame of being pregnant at the now age of sixteen. It was September 4, 2005, that my baby girl was born to an unwed mother and a father who was locked away in jail. When I looked into her eyes, I felt guilt and shame. I wasn't ready, but I knew one thing was for certain, I would do my very best to guarantee she would know that she was loved. She didn't have the easiest childhood. She watched me struggle to stay in school and to continue playing ball, but she also has watched me overcome many obstacles and never give up. I graduated from high school in 2007 with her by my side. I chose not to go off to college to play basketball, which I really loved. I couldn't imagine leaving her to feel the way that I felt growing up. I didn't want her to live without me being right there every minute of her life. So I decided to start out at a Jr college but after some time I transferred to a University.

Soon after I met my husband, we dated for a short period of time and decided to get married. Many people thought we were foolish and that things would end quickly for us. Just like any other marriage, we experienced trials and tribulations along the way, but we persevered. We have been married for nine years and still counting, we have had three more children. I can proudly say that I graduated from Lonestar College with my Associate's degree in 2014. I also graduated from Sam Houston State University in 2017 with my Bachelor's degree and I also have my teaching certificate to teach anywhere in the great state of Texas.

It took me ten years to achieve those goals and although I was a teenage mother and life was not always easy, I made a decision to be the best that I could be in life and to never give up. No matter what may come up in life as stumbling blocks, it is up TO ME to take those blocks and build them into something great. My daughter is now twelve years old and I cannot imagine where my life would have taken me if she had not come along and saved me. Understand that like me, God also has a plan for your life. This test you are being faced with now will soon become your testimony. Keep pushing, because giving up is not an option. NO! You can't change the past, but you can go forth knowing that God loves you and YOU ARE STILL SOMEBODY!!!

~Chanistie Wiley

CHAPTER 8

I WASN'T READY

Everything I've ever wanted, I had. Everything I've ever needed was given to me. I didn't have a thing to worry about. My family was always so loving and supportive. I graduated at the top of my class with a full scholarship to a Florida university. This girl was ready. Everything was set. Life was perfect.

But then…. I fell in love. I fell in love with a guy that was so charming and so sweet. Reminding me of the one man who had always given me his last, who had always loved me for me, who had always treated me like a Queen. He reflected my grandfather. I fell deeply in love with a guy who was everything I'd ever imagine. And then the shenanigans started. You start claiming his last name, doodling it on every paper, changing your Myspace name to match his so everyone knows you're together because of course…the world needs to know. It was bitter sweet because, in the process of gaining something so amazing, I lost my friends. I was okay with that. "First comes love, and then comes marriage. Then comes the baby in the baby carriage." It didn't exactly happen that way, but it happened.

At the age of 20, my life changed drastically. As I walked into Walgreens to purchase a pregnancy test, my heart dropped into the pits of my stomach. I couldn't swallow. I couldn't make it home. So, I stood in line trembling internally with fear. I couldn't help but have mixed emotions. I made my purchase and then made my way to the bathroom. I could hear the disappointing lectures from everyone who believed in me, the silent cries from those who were counting on me and the snickers from those who have been waiting and plotting on me to fail. Everything had changed moments after taking the test. I couldn't go back. I couldn't change what was to come.

Two fainted lines appeared on the test screen. I fumbled through the directions to make certain of the result but deep inside, it had already been confirmed. My body was still but I felt like I was moving 100 mph. I was baffled. How? Why now? Are you sure? As I walked to my car, all I could think about was my life. It was over. No school, no hanging out, no traveling. Nothing. Everything was about to change. To be honest, I wasn't ready for it. I wasn't ready to give up my perfect life. I wasn't ready to split my measly $10 an hour income with someone else. That money was for hair, nails, and clothes. I'm only 20.

At five months, the results from my tests came back. "Ms. Lawrence, your test came back positive. We will need to do further examinations to determine what is going on with the baby," said the doctor. My heart sank and if I wasn't sitting down, I probably would have collapsed. As my boyfriend sat across from me, I could see his eyes drop to the floor. It was then that I realized that I had become a mother. It was at that moment of declining to do an amniocentesis that I realized the unconditional love I had for my unborn child. No sickness, illness or genetic disorder would keep me from her. My faith was being tested. "All is well" were the words that I heard Him speak into my life while in prayer one morning. I held onto those words tighter than a person hanging off a cliff. It was the only thing that made me feel as though everything was going to be alright despite what it looked like.

Fast forward to February 19, 2012, around 3:00 A.M., it hit me. An uncontrollable pain and discomfort had taken over my body that I could not explain. My boyfriend rushed me to the hospital with no expectations that today was going to be the day. I dilated three centimeters and the nurse said, "You're gonna have this baby today." My initial emotions had emerged. I was only 21 and I was not ready to be a mother. My life hadn't even started, but the contractions came intensely minute after minute regardless of how I was feeling. As I rocked in that hospital bed from side to side, I tried to find a perfect position but I couldn't.

Hours had passed by and the pain started to grow. In a room, so cold I was burning. One hand grabbing my mother for comfort while yelling for someone to fan me with the other. I was irritated and miserable. At 8:00 P.M., the doctors rushed in, set up and only three people were left in the room. It was quiet and I was terrified. I begged for the epidural but it was too late so with no pain medication and four pushes later, I held the most beautiful creation I had ever laid my eyes on, Amber. I held her close to my chest as our heartbeats were on the same tune. I cried tears of happiness and tears of fear. Late nights and early mornings sound cliché right? Well, that's exactly what my life consisted of. After everyone was gone from the visits during the day, I was up and restless. I had support but a mother's job is never done.

Five months after giving birth, I was pregnant again...with Amy. I didn't understand it. I started to be upset with God. I started to question Him about His plan for my life because, at this point, I didn't know what that was anymore. Fast forward to two years later, I welcomed baby Amanda. My husband was enthused and excited about our family but I was over it. Once again, I was angry and this time hurt. My emotions were a complete wreck and post-partum depression was the only way I could explain how I felt on a regular basis. But ladies, Jeremiah 29:11 says, "For I know the plans I have for you, declares the LORD, plans for welfare and not for evil, to give you a future and a hope."

I know that what it looks like now is not what you've imagined. God is strategic and the audience of people watching you to either succeed or to fail is all for His glory. Your story, just like mines, will help to win a soul over to Christ. You are going to have to push through and fight even when you don't want too. You are going to have to fight and push through even when you don't have anything left in you. If I would have given up, I would not have founded Play Dates With Purpose. A platform that allows me to lead other young mothers like yourself to God through one on one and group mentoring.

I am still working on my life and trying to put all the pieces together but I want to encourage you to own your story. You've got to walk by faith, be willing to be saved by grace and understand that you are cherished by God.

~Nefertiria Toussaint

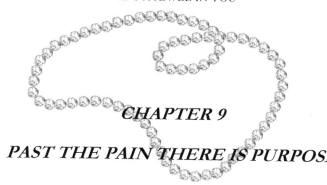

CHAPTER 9

PAST THE PAIN THERE IS PURPOSE

My journey into parenthood was undoubtedly framed from events endured during my childhood. I became a mother earlier than I had ever imagined or planned. In secret, I was in search of an unconditional love, an opportunity for me to give and to receive. However, love was already there, never failing, but I did not know it, or truly believed that I had even been exposed to it. In my quest or search for something believed unknown, I endured rough times. I was not even my biggest fan, co-signing with others and the adversary that I was not worthy. In addition, being told as a child that I was the product of an affair only helped sealed my faulty thought process. If I could give you a glimpse of my journey from the age of twelve and up into my adult years, you would see what I came to call my MADD BLAST. A journey that dealt with molestation, anxiety, depression, domestic abuse, broken relationships, low self-esteem, abortion, suicide and teen pregnancy. These were several pivotal points in my life that made me who I am today but they didn't define me; here I will give a glimpse of my journey.

At the age of twelve, my life was reshaped by my uncle, who committed the unspeakable, aggressive and sinful act of molestation. He decided to add pain to my journey early on. I felt guilty and wondered what I did to cause this. It left me feeling destroyed, and ultimately as an adult, wondering who I could have been or would have been, if not endured. As time went on, I continued to be lost as a child, in search of love and approval. Fast forward to a major life altering event for love, I became a teenage mother at the age of seventeen. I remember the moment I found out I was with child, as the old folks often stated it. I was in the emergency room, waiting on test results only to confirm the inevitable. I sat there thinking of what the possibilities were of me being pregnant and how it would be, but in the back of my mind I knew there was no other explanation for the clock like work of morning sickness. Also, wondering what possessed me to answer no to the doctor when he asked if I was sexually active. The doctor re-entered the room with the response, well it's a miracle, you are pregnant. My sister who sat with me patiently the entire time, provided encouraging words that everything would be okay no matter what, only to return a frightful glance once the doctor confirmed the already knowing. I knew what my sister was thinking, mama will not be happy about this. There I was the third of her offspring set-up to be a statistic, just another unwed, teenage mother.

Once I knew, I was with child, I declared it would be a girl and I would name her Ashley. I could finally give and get love in return. Eventually, I would birth three more children, Keshawn, Sierra, and Sanzara. For now, I was still in high-school, but due to my pregnancy, I had to be re-zoned to an alternative school. This was somewhat of a relief from the laughs, sneers, and whispers in school, but eventually only to endure the same from members of my family. So, I set my sites on a journey to prove to everyone that I was somebody, not a failure, and would not be ridiculed, boy was I confused. I had a good start. I graduated high school on time despite my challenges. I got my first apartment a few months before I turned eighteen, I had a great job, reliable car, but of course, immaturity remains instilled in me. At this point in my life, I was still driven to prove others wrong, but I didn't realize what I thought was a strength was a weakness.

As time went on and further wrong corners turned, I found myself in a familiar place. At this point, still a very young mother, I was homeless with my children, trading off the opportunity on rather to sleep in my Oldsmobile or in a well-chosen abandoned house. This went on for months, and I remember sitting in a soup kitchen, pondering on what to do next. What was so ironic was that a few tables away I saw my drug addicted aunt partaking of the same meal, but I made sure not to allow our glances from our plates to be met. As my poor choices became critical, I decided to give them up and it was the hardest thing I've ever done in my life. I felt I had no other choices or people to turn to. That night, I slept in my car at the cemetery, where my father was buried, feeling more lost than ever. I had to look at where I was and where I was going. I was a mother of four children by the age of 23, three from my previous marriage and one from a second failed marriage. I found myself in a continuum pursuit for love and happiness, if they really accompanied each other. I still couldn't get it right and did not understand why. I had hit rock bottom, at least that's what I thought but I had not reached the pit just yet. I still had no identity; to others maybe but not to myself. I still had a long journey ahead, but against chosen odds and what was told to me, I found the love of Jesus, and I prevailed.

Life started to turn around thanks to God's grace and mercy. My path was turning because I had found that unconditional love, the love that only Jesus could give. Although I was now a single mom, I graduated from college, started my nursing career at the age of 26, and bought my first house at the age of 28. I continued to learn more about whom I was and what God had in store for me. My heart was open and I had no doubt that my mother Cornelia Houston

Mason and my father Charles David Houston, cherished and loved me. I lost them both by the age of 29, but I knew they were and are proud of me. Although my birth parents are not earthly present, I am grateful for the love of my paternal grandmother, Lucille Tanksley, who is never more than a call away to laugh, love and pray with me. I thank her for helping me stay grounded in Christ. There have been so many other blessings, friends, loved ones and accomplishments that I am grateful for. I am more than certain anyone going through similar or more events can do the same. Today, you can see a dynamic woman of God with a secure, strong identity and a knowing purposeful journey. What I endured, I learned from it. I re-channeled the hate, the disappointments, the failures and the pain. I am a proud wife, with a terrific husband, a mother, and grandmother instilling an identity principle into my children, my friends, and those I meet. I thank God, for His love, the maturation process, and continued growth. My continued plight to prove myself was no longer needed. My requests now are not so much as helping me Lord, but my Lord uses me to help others.

When the words of the Lord ring out to you that is when the true meaning of everything working out for the good of those who love the Lord will be so clear. My further encouragement to you, we all have a purpose that hibernates in us, understanding that God has chosen us all for a determined mission reveals the path one should take. There's an opportunity to be re-shaped, re-born and re-named by God, but we first must get to know Him. In Jesus, you can receive unconditional love that never measures up to what man will offer. I say push forward, full speed ahead in seeking God's plan for your life; through faith and belief, it's obtainable. YOU HAVE A PURPOSE! A lost soul that is introduced to the love of Jesus is a joy that cannot be explained but definitely experienced.

~Charley Willis

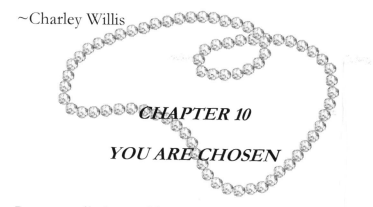

CHAPTER 10

YOU ARE CHOSEN

I never called myself a teen mother. It wasn't because I was ashamed or had feelings of regret. I believe it had more to do with the label of "teen mother". You see when society calls you a "teen mother", they instantly get the image of a young lady who is being "fast". They say she was out there showing her tail and got herself pregnant, knocked up, or in the family way. They put a scarlet T on your spirit that makes you want to hold your head down in shame. Although teen mothers aren't anything new, coming from an upper middle-class professional family, being a teen mother was not what I chose as my destiny.

My teen mother story began not because I was fast or promiscuous. I was just a typical girl, 14, on her first date and he was a guy I had been talking on the phone with for a few months. The day went fine until something went horribly wrong. Despite my insistence by saying no and that I wasn't quite ready, I was violated. I vividly remember the moment I was forced to have sex against my will. You see, if I chose to call myself a teen mother, I was going to have to explain what happened to me to make me a teen mom and I was not prepared to forgive him or myself.

Even as a teenager, when I explain how I got pregnant, the revelation always changed the atmosphere. The look in the eyes of the person hearing this news turned from stoic judge to deer in the headlights. It is like they are trying to rationalize or decipher the concept that a girl could be a teen mother without being promiscuous. Being called a teen mother felt like I would be subjected to a lifetime of judgment as soon as they heard the words. Acknowledging and accepting the title of teen mom meant I did a crime and was sentenced to a life of being a statistic.

Don't get me wrong. Everyone in some way is a statistic. We all are subjected to some kind of data that is gathered for the distinct purposes of documenting history, observing trends and shaping society. Statistical data gathering and labeling are a necessity. My issues are the attitudes from the stereotypes based on those statistics. According to statistical data, many of the stats about me are considered negative. I am black, female, teen mother, divorced, previously bankrupt, blended family and obese. Now ain't that a mouth full? For the average person in the United States, my labels say I am destined to a life of poverty, regret, shame, sorrow, and struggle. Guess what… The devil is a LIE!.

My journey of peace came with many struggles. Unfortunately, most my of struggles were self-imposed. Internally, I allowed my statistics and labels of teen motherhood to affect the way I treated myself. After I gave birth, I became numb. I was drowning in doubt, rage and shame. My value system was fueled by my overall perception that no one cared about my experience of having a baby at such a young age or that fact that I was raped. In my eyes, everyone was interested in how they were affected by my pregnancy instead of counseling me or comforting me. I focused so much on having someone else's validation and defending my name that I got lost in despair, which lead to unhealthy behaviors. My reactions formed a position of shame that caused me too adversely act out and do things unbecoming to my true character. I was in a cycle of self-imposed punishments such as negative talk, isolation, promiscuity and even feelings of unworthiness.

You must see past your statistic. You can't change the past, but you can decide to live on purpose for the future. My first step to overcoming was to decide to live with joy and peace. It's just that simple. You can either wallow in the details of how circumstances have ruined your life, discredited your name or even turn people against you. Or you can decide to claim your rightful place as an heir of God who has already conquered doubt, shame, fear and death for you. My decision wasn't easy, so many times my emotions tried to overtake my heart's desire to forgive and be happy. On the outside, I appeared to be handling my new season of life gracefully, yet on the inside, I was enraged by the sheer fact that I had to go through this season. These negative stereotypes were so powerful in my journey to surrendering to Jesus.

At age 20, I was tired of not feeling worthy of love. In my logical mind, there had to be a reason God let me be a teen mother. I began to search the Bible for answers. Then it hits me. I had to forgive. I had to stop beating myself up. With prayer, I discovered I was created to be my daughter's mother; me no one else. I was the one who God chose to show His unconditional love to her. I was chosen. At that point, it became more important for me to show my daughter God's love than it did for me to wallow in self-despair. I had to let her know she was loved not only by me but also mostly by God. I changed the narrative. My statistic became my testimony. My daughter saved me from being a bitter woman regretting life to a true follower of Jesus. She became my first disciple and the first person I would bring to Christ. If I had not been a teen mother, I may never have experienced the purest love in this world; the love of a mother and child and the love of God in my life. It took years for me to understand that I am worthy and valued regardless of what "they" say. I am a jewel; a precious stone that shines with God's grace and love.

My name is Shennice Cleckley, I am 43 years old and I became a mother for the first time when I gave birth to my beautiful daughter at the age of 15. My life is full of joy, kindness, forgiveness, and love. I love my life and I regret no parts of it.

~Shennice Pruitt-Cleckley

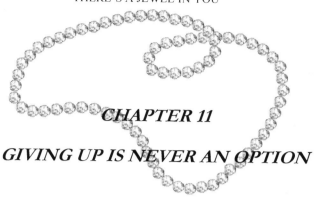

CHAPTER 11

GIVING UP IS NEVER AN OPTION

It was the summer of 94' when it happened and I was scared to death. How in the world was this going to work? What would my parents say? What would other people say? How could I have allowed this to happen? What about sports? I played basketball, softball and ran track? What in the world, am I going to do now? No one is supposed to be a mother at the age of fifteen.

Growing up, I was a daddy's girl. I absolutely adored my father and there was no doubt that he felt the same way about me. My brother and I grew up for the first half of our lives with both parents in the household. We were middle-class Americans. Our father was in the Army and our mother worked for NASA. They worked hard to make sure we had the things that they didn't have growing up in the South. We moved from California to Mississippi when I was about ten and that's when our lives began to change.

Our parents got a divorce and I felt abandoned. My father was no longer at home with us and the military did what it does best...he went TDY stateside and overseas. Now, what was this daddy's girl to do? The only man I had known to love me was not where I wanted him to be. He was not at home, so there became a void in my life that I felt needed to be filled and that is exactly what I did. I found myself secretly liking boys because I could not date them. My mother was strict and if my brother could not go then it was a no.

I do not even remember how I met my child's father but I believe it started maybe in the 7th or 8th grade. We called ourselves dating at school and secretly talking on the phone. Writing love letters to each other. Somewhere along the way, I found myself in love even though I had no meaning of the word. I stood my ground at first with no sex. I knew it was wrong and I knew the consequences of it. I had classmates who had become pregnant and I did not want to end up like that. I wanted to play sports. It was one of the ways I was able to get out of the house and see my friends. I did not want a baby, but my desire to please him was greater.

After continuously being asked in love letters and on the phone, I found myself in the position doing what I said I did not want to do before marriage. He had my heart, but it was not enough. Everyone was doing it, including him with other girls, but he was not doing it with me. I was the challenge. I was the outsider that no one had been with. I was blinded by infatuation disguised as love. After the first time and nothing happened, it seemed to be okay. After all, we were in love or at least I was and that is what people do when they are in love. Right?

It was finals week our freshmen year in high school. Everyone planned hook-ups during finals because we did not have to be at school the whole day. We only had certain finals to take but our parents thought we had full days. We planned our "DATE" along with another couple and then our lives began to change. I went on summer vacation and when I missed my period, I immediately knew I was pregnant. I did not tell anyone and went on as if nothing was wrong. The entire time, my mind is in a whirlwind. How long would I be able to hide it?

When I returned home, I never said a word to my mother. I just continued to go on with life. When school started in August, so did softball and I played as if no one was growing on the inside of me. In the back of mind, I wondered what would happen if I got hurt or if I had to slide into base. What in the world was I going to do?

It did not take long for my mother to figure it out and one of the first things she said was, "No more sports!" I was devastated. Sports was my life! Forget the fact that I had a baby growing on the inside of me. I wanted to play sports. We were in a tournament at home and I had to miss the game. I did not call my coach or anyone to let me know I was not going to be there. When I got the call to see why I was not at the tournament, I told them I was sick. It hurt to have to tell my coaches why I could no longer play. I had become the one thing that I said I was not going to be...A STATISTIC!

At this time, my father was stationed in Turkey and I had to deliver the news that his baby girl was having a baby. I was scared and did not know what to expect. I did not know what he would say. How did an honor roll student find herself in such a situation? I remember when I told my boyfriend I was pregnant; I got no response on the other side of the phone. It was not long before we broke up and I realized that it had all been a game to him. I was no longer his love. He moved on to the next one.

The one I was so in love with became the one I hated even more. I hated the fact that I had to raise this baby, while it appeared he got off scotch free. I had to give up sports while he was still able to play. I was the one everyone talked about as if I did this by myself. I was the one who was blamed for becoming pregnant. It was all my fault. My emotions could not handle it but I had to grow up fast. There was no time to deal with my feelings because I had a baby to raise.

I had a decision to make regardless of what everyone was saying about me. I had to choose to NOT GIVE UP! I had to make the choice to NOT become what the statistics say I would become. I made up in my mind that not only would I make it but my daughter would too. While I was out for about six weeks, I made sure that I did all my work. I would not let anything keep me from graduating on time. My parents and my brother were supportive in making sure everything was together. My daughter did not have to want for anything. Her granny was always in her life as well as her other great uncles and aunts on her father's side. My daughter always knew she was loved no matter what! To be quite honest, she was spoiled rotten and still is today.

I was always told that I had to live for my daughter and every decision I made had to be about her. In doing that, I lost myself. I did not know who I was or what I was capable of becoming. All I knew and lived was to be a mother to my daughter. I didn't' have an identity outside of that and because I did not know who I was, I went searching again in all the wrong places. Upon entering college in the fall of '97, it was the first time I was away from my daughter.

A new environment with no mommy duties and no sense of identity was a dangerous place for me. There were so many young men to choose from and no one said there was a limit. It is only by God's grace that I only have one child. My first two years in college were definitely a revelation for me. I was on the brink of failing out and no one knew about it. I had to get myself together fast, quick and in a hurry. It was not until my junior year when I brought my daughter to school with me and got my first apartment, did I start to realize, just how important my decisions were for the both of us. I graduated in '02 with my B.A. in Business Administration and again in '05 with my B.S. in Culinary Arts.

Today my daughter is a college graduate and off to graduate school! God has kept us and He is keeping you. Don't ever give up! No matter how hard it gets or who talks about you, keep pressing forward! Your circumstances do not determine your destiny. They are just stepping-stones to your GREATER! You can go from a statistic to a SUCCESS, but it takes hard work, perseverance, and resilience to get there. Go ahead, look in the mirror, and tell yourself, **"I Am Still Somebody and Giving Up Is Never An Option!"**

~Chantea Williams

#PRAYER10 MOVEMENT

#PRAYER10 started out as a 30 day prayer challenge but now it is a movement to remind us to spend 10 minutes a day in prayer with God. Luke 5:16 states, "And he withdrew himself into the wilderness, and prayed." Jesus understood the necessity of prayer in His life and it is recorded many times in the bible where He left His disciples to go pray.

We are often so busy with our schedules that we end up scheduling God right out of our lives. Our weekly worship services aren't enough to keep us on this Christian journey. We need a personal relationship with God which requires us to spend personal time with Him daily.

Unfortunately, too many people don't believe that they have time to spend with God. They believe that they need hours at a time when all they need is 10 minutes a day. You would be surprised how only 10 minutes a day will make such a positive change in your life.

There have already been numerous people reporting how #PRAYER10 is changing their life! We are totally excited to hear this wonderful news. This is the whole point of this movement. To encourage the people of God to get back to one of the basics of our faith which is prayer.

There are t-shirts available for the entire family so be sure to order yours today at www.greaterwomen.com. We look forward to hearing how #PRAYER10 is impacting your life. Please share your stories by emailing us at info@greaterwomen.com.

I Am Still Somebody™

This is our teen mom mentoring program where we are ***Encouraging, Empowering & Equipping Teen Moms To Be Greater Mothers and Greater Women***. I know first-hand what it feels like to be a teen mom, with all the negativity that is typically associated with it. Our goal as a ministry is to provide teen moms with the knowledge and tools to beat the odds against them.

Our program, which can also be done virtually, is to get teen moms focused and directed on the right track. We will provide free webinars on various topics to help teen moms heal emotionally and address those difficult issues in their life. We also offer valuable life skills they need to achieve greater accomplishments.

We also provide workshops and sessions for organizations that work with teen moms or have a desire to do so. If your organization is interested in hosting a workshop, webinar or ordering books, please email us at info@iamstillsomebody.com.

If you would like to donate to this program you may do so by visiting **www.iamstillsomebody.com** and clicking on the donation link. We appreciate your donation to help us reach as many teen mothers as possible and to help end the cycle. The next time you see a teen mom please remind them that they are STILL SOMEBODY!

The program is tentatively scheduled to launch in 2018.

I AM STILL SOMEBODY™ SERIES

I AM STILL SOMEBODY™

I AM STILL SOMEBODY™: WORKBOOK

I AM STILL SOMEBODY™: PRAYER BOOK

I AM STILL SOMEBODY™: PRAYER JOURNAL

To order the book series or an official I Am Still Somebody™ t-shirt visit our website **www.iamstillsomebody.com.** Discount pricing is available for bulk orders of 10 or more on books only.

Meet the Authors

*S*hakkyra Austin a native of Ridgely, Maryland is a mother, student, inspiring author, and servant of God. She is one of the leading ladies in the outreach ministry for her home church Kingdom Vision Family Worship Center.

Miss Austin received salvation at the age of eighteen and has been on a spiritual journey to live for the Lord ever since.

Her gentle spirit, lifestyle, and servitude to her children (natural and spiritual) are her greatest witnesses. Shakkyra Austin lives in Harrington, DE, with her sons, who she is extremely proud of.

*J*oy C. Avery, M.Ed. is the mother of four young adults. Her first son was born when she was only 16 years old. While enduring a difficult marriage for 13 years, Joy managed to publish a novel, earn a bachelor's degree in Business Administration and begin a career as an educator. After divorce, she went on to earn a Master's Degree in Educational Leadership. Joy transitioned from a career in education to being a full-time entrepreneur. She is a real estate professional who also educates people in the areas of financial empowerment and business development. She is a faithful servant in her local church and dedicated to encouraging and developing people.

*R*onda Braden is a single mother of 6 adult children. She has 5 wonderfully awesome grandchildren with whom she loves to spend her free time. Ronda is an advocate for grandparents and their participation (interaction) in the lives of their grandchildren. It is because of an awesome relationship with her own grandmother, that she feels so passionately about this. Ronda aspires to one day have a nonprofit organization addressing this very important issue. Ronda has been a Billing/Payroll Specialist for 20+ years with a medical staffing agency. She has also received her Associates Degree from St. Louis Community College and is working towards obtaining her Bachelors in Business Administration. She is also an active member in her local church as well as on the state level assisting with recordkeeping, health unit and usher board. Ronda also offers excellent VA services to several entrepreneurs from various backgrounds. ~ Your Business' Greatest Asset~

*S*hennice Pruitt-Cleckley *is a former Policy Director turned award winning baker and serial entrepreneur celebrating her 14th year in business. Like many women, Shennice wears many hats. She's a baker, author, business and relationship coach. "My passion is to help women who want to leap but are scared; to empower and support Mompreneurs who need someone that understands this season in life; to encourage couples who want to learn to love each other better. I see you and I am here to serve your needs." While her career is very important, being a wife and mother are her greatest joys.*

In 2017, Shennice authored her first children's book, "Please Wait Mommy's Working" based on her real life experience as a Mompreneur. As a speaker, Shennice's enthusiastic, conversational tone positively empowers audiences to move forward and take action. Shennice's style of coaching emphasizes accountability for milestones missed or hit through strategies tailored to achieve specific goals. Shennice resides in Columbia, SC, with her husband LeBrian. Together they have 4 children and 1 grandchild. Shennice works in the community by serving on various boards including 2 terms on the City of Columbia Accommodations Tax And What's Next Midlands. She is a member of Zeta Phi Beta Sorority Inc. and Junior League of Columbia.

*T*ammie Lavern Jackson is a 46 year old mother of nine & proud Nana to nine grandchildren, Ke'mori (RIP). Deveon (9), Joseph Jr. (8), Na'Riyah (6), Jermaine (6), Amiya (4), Kevin (3), Javon (2) & Jordyn (21 months). Ms. Jackson is the Founder of Giving Backs Packs Miami- Team S.S. United, a non-profit organization dedicated to feeding the homeless and providing backpacks filled with food, clothes, personal care items, as well as school supplies to needy families and individuals. Precious Pearls of God Women's Mentoring Program, a non-profit group that provides support and mentors to women of all ages and backgrounds. She is also the Owner of Four Brothers & A Sister Accounting and Tax Services as well as Sword & Shield Security Services. Ms. Jackson currently resides in Miami Gardens, Florida.

*A*shley Thomas, the mother to the most amazing daughter A'talia Nicole. Entrepreneur, motivational speaker and author for women, teen moms and kids at risk. Not for one second did my achievements come without great pain and sacrifice. I've overcome the many challenges of a teen pregnancy by the grace of God. After a few years of working under the constraints of the corporate environment and longing to express my creative side on a larger scale, at age 26 I launched Fire Ant Marketing. That led me to share my story through various platforms and speaking engagements. I have turned what seemed like a mess into a message that will serve, motivate and inspire others.

Nefertiria Toussaint is a 27-year-old wife to Marvens Toussaint and mother to three beautiful girls; Amber Faith, Amy Grace and Amanda Cherish. She is currently living in Miami, Florida, and studying Early Childhood Education. Nefertiria is a passionate individual and entrepreneur who founded Play Dates With Purpose, which is a nonprofit organization that empowers, educates and encourages teenage mothers in the community through one on one and group mentoring sessions.

C hanistie Smith-Wiley is a native of Conroe Texas. She became a teenage parent at the age of 16 and despite her circumstances she didn't let that stop her. She is now the mother of 4 children, 2 daughters and 2 sons; and is a loving and devoted wife. She also is the founder and owner of My Craft House Designs, a small craft/t-shirt business. After a decade she is now pursuing her teaching dreams and hopes to be able to coach high school girls' basketball one day. She is an active member of Just Church Ministries. This is her first experience with writing a book; she is overjoyed about this experience and cannot wait to see where this journey leads her.

*C*alandra Williams lives in North Texas with her husband Culus Williams II and their three children. She is an inspirational speaker, Christian blogger, mentor, and author. She is young and radical, and passionate about kingdom building. Calandra is the Co-Founder of Truth Written Ministries. Through her testimonies, she hopes to inspire someone to discover their purpose, passion, and power. When Calandra is not out changing lives, she enjoys singing, dancing, reading, and spending quality time with her family.

*C*hantea M. Williams is a chef, author, speaker and mentor, who loves encouraging the people of God to become greater through the word of God. Through her gifts, God created the Greater Working Women Ministries, where they strive to encourage, empower and equip women from all walks of life to live out their God given purpose with holy boldness. She also is the Founder & CEO of I Am Still Somebody™, a teen mom mentoring program. As a former teen mom at the age of 15, Chantea understands the issues that teen mothers face and feels compels to teach them how to transform their mindset and their situations will follow. In this program teen moms will learn valuable life skills that will propel them from a statistic to a SUCCESS. The program is scheduled to launch in 2018. She has written two volumes of The Greater Working Woman Devotional, a 30-day devotional to inspire women to cultivate their relationship with God, themselves and with people. She has also released volume one of The Greater Working Woman Prayer Book, a 30 day prayer book to ignite the prayer lives *of women. The Prayer10 movement was birthed out of her passion to pray and to encourage people to spend at least 10 minutes a day praying to God. Chantea is also the proud mother of Kiana Williams. You can sign up for Greater Working Women Ministries' monthly newsletter at www.greaterwomen.com for upcoming events and product releases.*

THERE'S A JEWEL IN YOU

*C*harlesetta *Willis* (Charley*)* *is a wife, mother, registered nurse, aspiring entrepreneur and author. Her life experiences have led her to strive further in moving herself and others toward loving oneself and their truths based on the word of God. Her works are through motivating, mentoring, coaching, and counseling. As an ordained minister, in her local church Destiny Worship Center, she is the Ministry of Helps leader, as well as, the Marriage Ministry along with her husband. She has been working in the healthcare industry for over 25 years in a vast of therapeutic areas. Her nursing career involves healthcare management, pharmaceutical research, allied healthcare speaking, consulting, as well as research publications. She employs a holistic view of a health model, which includes aspects of one's spiritual, mental, and physical well-being, based upon living 7 Dimensionally Well.*

COMING SOON!

There's A Jewel In You Collection

Volume 2

We are now accepting applications for Volume II. If you were a mother between the ages of 13-21 and you would like to share your story, then this is the perfect opportunity! We will only be selecting 12 women for this project so don't delay in submitting your application.

Here are the application requirements of the anthology:

1. $50 registration fee (non-refundable) due upon acceptance.

2. A professional headshot in PNG format. (NO EXCEPTIONS)

3. Website (if you don't have one then you have to agree to have one created prior to submitting your first draft.)

This is an amazing opportunity to become a published author or add another book to your resume. This movement is changing the lives of young mothers across the world. This project is no walk in the park. You will have to manage your time wisely and participate in the group discussions. Submit your application today at www.iamstillsomebody.com and we look forward to sharing your story with the world.

Made in the USA
Columbia, SC
02 September 2017